To the New World
VALERIE DUFF

salmonpoetry

Published in 2010 by
Salmon Poetry
Cliffs of Moher, County Clare, Ireland
Website: www.salmonpoetry.com
Email: info@salmonpoetry.com

Copyright © Valerie Duff, 2010

ISBN 978-1-907056-28-4

All rights reserved. No part of this publication may be reproduced or transmitted in any form or by any means, electronic or mechanical, including photography, recording, or any information storage or retrieval system, without permission in writing from the publisher. The book is sold subject to the condition that it shall not, by way of trade or otherwise, be lent, resold or otherwise circulated without the publisher's prior consent in any form of binding or cover other than that in which it is published and without a similar condition, including this condition, being imposed on the subsequent purchaser.

Cover artwork: *Canvas-Wrapped Hull, Boatyard Series* © 2008 Emily Hiestand
www.ehiestand.com
www.elementsboston.net/about/emily.htm

Cover design & typesetting: *Siobhán Hutson*
Printed in England by imprint*digital*.net

*for Jacob
Northanna
and Ernest Marlowe*

Acknowledgements

Thanks are due to the editors of the following magazines in which some of these poems first appeared:

AGNI, Antioch Review, Bostonia, Denver Quarterly, Harvard Review, Outsiders Anthology (Milkweed Press)*, PN Review, Saint Ann's Review, Salamander, Verse, Zoland Poetry Anthology* (Steerforth Press).

And to the editors of the following websites: AGNI.com, Isle.com, and Perihelion (WebDelSol).

I am indebted to Yeats' "Sailing to Byzantium" which provides the impetus for "To the New World" (and the line "consume my heart away").

The italicized text in "In the Name of the Lord" comes from *The Journals of George Fox*.

The italicized text in "Illness Makes an Agreeable Variety" comes from Keats' letters.

Thanks to those who helped with these poems: thanks to Jennifer Barber, Remy Holzer Kirsch, Jake Strautmann, Cheryl Follon, Jennifer Lowe, Harry Clifton, Gerald Dawe, Brendan Kennelly, Derek Walcott, Robert Pinsky, Rosanna Warren, Fred Marchant, Lucie Brock-Broido, Stephen Dobyns, Louise Glück, Don Share, Wyn Cooper, Amy Gehman, Claudia Emerson, Dr. James Locke, and thanks also for the ongoing support of my mother and family. Thanks to the Massachusetts Cultural Council and St. Botolph Foundation for their financial support.

And thanks to the memory of Liam Rector and to the memory of my father, Ernest Arthur Duff, without whom this book would not be.

Contents

I

After Dinner	11
In the Name of the Lord	12
Traveling Salesman	13
Backwoods	14
Builder	15
Evidence	16
Road Turns to Road	17
Flames	18
Self-Portrait with Household Items	19
Plateau	20
White Space	21
No Vacancy	22
To the New World	23

II

Name Desire	27
Akhmatova to her Husband in Russia	28
Odysseus with a Siren in the Corner of His Eye	29
Russian Chapter	30
Halo	31
Proverb	32
The Way Light Travels	33
The Nymphs, Seeing Circe at the Table	35
Song for the Oarsman	36
The Kiss	37
Speak Back	38
Letters from an Exile	39
The Road to Hell is Paved with	40
Tornado Alley	41
Kept	42

George Sand's Invitation to Her Lover	44
Urban Blue	45
Little Opera	46
Manhattan	47

III

Legend	51
Lughnasa	52
The Curator Explains	53
The Ferry North to Isle of Mull	54
Gospel	55
Viking	57
Waterfront	58
Tell You	59
Before the Monks, Attempts at Confession	60
The Mill Wheel	61
Illness Makes an Agreeable Variety	62
The Shepherd	63
View on the Arno: Coming About	64
Year after Year	65
Brooklyn	66
Composition	67
Critical	68
Recess	69
Intaglio	70
The Booby	72
Author Biography	75

I

After Dinner

I was raised by a big black
lady named Rose.
Every dinner, which we called supper,
we'd face off, my elbows on the table,
her elbows on the table, her black
eyes, slightly red, on my blue,
slightly red. A flat slab
of red meat bleeding
before me. It was almost time for bed.
We sat hours with the beef
as it slobbered in the beans
and cold carrots. The ice cream
in the ice box stayed there. I should have known
this, but I was
a white child with a will. I was Rose's
little girl, walked a bear
my brother gave me
in a doll
carriage round the suburbs. All the mothers
on their porches gurgled *What's her name,*
Sweetheart? Look at your pretty
blond hair. I called her April
because it was April.
Sweetheart.
I was six
and hit my best friend with a hoe.
Now I don't know
where Rose went, though April's
in the basement
of my parents' house. I eat
in New England, date men
who ask me out to dinner:
What's your name, Sweetheart?
Look at your pretty blond hair...

In the Name of the Lord

Under maples dropping pollen, trace
Of honeys, powders, I made my journey
That spring *there was a distracted woman*
Under doctor's hand traveled far, from meeting-
House to meeting-house *about to let her blood,*
Being first bound listening to the people of the town.
Some could barely read or write. Most were farmers
Many people holding her by violence
Living off the sale of corn and wheat.
He could get no blood In fallow fields,
We sat, while women *with her hair*
Loose all about her ears quoted scripture.
I said nothing for awhile, wishing to be clear.
I desired them to unbind her.
They could not touch the spirit in her
By which she was tormented The town had never heard
Of our society. Some were wary
Of my company. *I was moved* I only wished
To speak to their condition *in the name*
Of the Lord somehow reveal the light within.
Many people took me in *bid her be quiet*
And she was. She mended and afterwards
Looking for my place, I pray
For patience *she received the Truth* and hope the heat
Will break. The crickets in the meadow lose their voice
Continued to her death until the breeze *the Lord's*
Name honoured races gently through the leaves *to whom the glory*
Then they sing out, fiercely in the swamps *of works belongs*

Traveling Salesman

A mountain girl, she earned him
as she listened at the door for the moment of attack,
scratched her claws on the bark
and brought down shavings.
A mountain girl, she earned him.

The scraps were pieced together in a cord.
Somewhere buried in the back
is a Wurlitzer which smells of oak and dirt
left in the woods for the crows,
the scraps all pieced together in a cord.

I don't even know if she wanted a child.
Especially in these days of insecurity,
familiar backwater and forward highway.
Or the sight of a child, a spit-shined cradle,
I don't know.

Backwoods

Flute and pastoral. Circle the dell, following shadows
   of a big, black bird,
and if I did, I'd go until I reached state lines. What I want
   and don't want, lives
here in the green of Virginia. A cat runs under the
   rusted car out back. *Curl up,*
Jackal. In a field next door, the cat lady claps her hands.
   She gives her kitty-yodel
and they fly in hundreds towards her lap, rub her apron.
   Pipe the flute, sing the pastoral.

These are our morals and heroes. Even in the dell, I knew
   I'd break the bars, the brisk
fall air, religion, deeply Southern. The redboard church.
   You could almost hear
hymns percolate inside its pores, snaking out, the streets
   filled with recorded bells.
I knew I'd head Northward through my own weather.

Leaves cover the windshield. On rides up-country,
   high-strung New York Thruway
goes from green to full-blown tapestry, bleak and back
   again in torment. Black tattoo
on the gas attendant's arm. The bronze hair, the pores of
   that arm. A child in the doorway
sucks his thumb, dressed in his bare feet. Gardens, dusk
   on Sunday.
I'm nothing more than this. A gate swings open, shut,
   open in the wind, listening
to her brocade prayer of *tabbytabbytabby* sung out that
   draws me in.

Builder

When the rafters spit their flaws out in the rain,
when the sky heaps snow,
the eaves a cistern wrapped in flannel,
snowfall falling pyramidal in a window hinge,
when the wind acts Roman,
fields cuttlebone, a stinging fist
retreating out of reach, shrilling *must have something*,
when the glare of sun on roof and ridge
hits the rabbit hole which waits
for rabbits, and blinks at the road
like a blackout

when you build yourself a house,
blow someone else's stories on the far wall
and whatever you do, do it well.

Evidence

I wonder how you are.

I drove to Dorchester, rain
stabbing the car, when it was dark,

saw a large gray cat step out
into the road. It was hit.

Broken, it danced. Electric rumba
I watched but couldn't bear to touch

the shock of movement, didn't stop.

Road Turns to Road

Wait. Dirt accumulates
at the delta, states
roll by, forsythia
and brown hills rifled

as if in sweat, tracing highways
broad and black with sun,
tarred, equivocal. Mountain
green, pre-spring, passes

through the rearview,
leering. Gentle, gentle
cities just beyond the curve,
one more roadside motel.

In dark oak bars, men
and pretty girls, even
in the middle of the day.
To play harmonica like that.

Lyrics no one else has heard.
Hearing it's like healing
from an accident, having trouble
standing. Deep in the woods,

foxes climb the hill. On each
side of the road, a jetty of ice
unmelted, clings against the turn
of tourists, carloads, conversation. Then

legacies of no one. At night,
maps of stars, murmurs,
indigenous names. Wait again.
The cloverleaf spins out in all directions.

Flames

for J. S.

Map the routes, hypothesize
how light jumps into water,
dives into the shortest line. The ocean's
garbled stretch towards light.

In 1609, Galileo deepens his work
on the telescope, sees bits of stars
beyond the moon
as if the earth were tapped.

Lean off the balcony for a cleaner look:
night scraped into the palm.

He holds the polished tube
as if to play a tune, and careful,
wipes the glass with cloth.

Each hairline fracture carries strain.
Chemical and flames, burning papers
tossed into the sink
become invention, *show me how.*

Self-Portrait with Household Items

Corner shop. Cellar rain. Buy two brushes,
bristles fresh from fields—
sunflower beds near the coast,
so flat the sea rises above them

and thatched roofs ripple.

When pushed through crowds,
buy fish.
Remember compassion,
render the world as it is—

image, pose, shoulder.

A leather-backed chair
scrubbed with oils,
pinched from the alley.
Pedestrian bridge over water.

Still life, be faithful.

Ocean comes back, the fish need ice,
a bit of wet in order not
to fall apart, detached,
on canvas. This accomplished,

Cezanne said, *be an apple*

basket on table, shift stool
and blanket. One thick
heel turned left. The trick
is to keep moving.

Open bottle, green fruit, yellow ray on brick mantle.

Plateau

I never learned how to tread
or float, but clung to bridle and bit

of Phaeton's horses, hard
but not heartless, as if to warrant

the plateau where the inner ear stops
spinning, and barometers

pulse out a stable surf. When asked what words
I spoke, I'll tell onlookers

that I put my hands around the air,
my lifeline, yanked to be pulled out

of the cold Atlantic,
hair matted

as if peat stuck the strands
from some ore-filled mountain shaft.

But I'll never tell the cut I wore,
the travel time it took, or how I memorized

your ankles in the foam,
looking to the bottom at the drift

and weed and anything that breathed down there.
The arc from toll to toll, the pine barrens.

White Space

This fall, let's change perspective, let's have
a jubilee. Change back the fact
that sorrow comes in shapes we can't manage.
Unrecognizable riffs roll out: bleak
ignorant phrases. I've begun to spout
gems of therapeutic art created by idiots
left in asylums to sit and make therapeutic art
as they moan and rock.
    Let me hold you in the bath,
cleansing you, like John the Baptist,
hollow and crying, the wilderness
buckling beneath autumn's weight. Like idealists-
gone-wrong, French revolutionaries torn
by disease and terror, tritone
of voices below the garret window, knife wielded
by a slip of a starving girl. Not pretty,
but in motion, shocked by personal revelation,
the kick to get off the crossroads. Outside, leaves
    put their fists through a sleeve,
bloody, lemoned, salted and soured like every emotion
I no longer let myself feel, first right, then left.
Like it's joyful. It's death
and there's not a damn thing to be done
but accept the fall. White space
coats crabapples, tight to the branch.
We'll inflict it on stems and berries
    while the world ends,
stall the record's firm direction,
finger on black glass, against the grain,
change back what you've revealed.
The animal skin removed to see
muscles underneath, carcass of a market fish,
salted and sunned. The body, in illness,
reworks itself. The trees won't drop
their leaves, they don't let go,
even in the rain. I hope
    that someone, something, whispers in your ear
    the way you whispered in mine: I'm dying, I'm lovely, I'm here.

No Vacancy

I don't want to be witness to this, undone
by supplication,

and every injured party on the news,
a loved one. I play again and again

this great indifference like a brick in the rain,
in the tide, a shore scraped into a crane,

like Louis Armstrong's trumpet
accented by its plummet down a mute, deep well,

the Golden Gate bloodshot between green banks,
a mentor disappearing in a cab,

and overhead, the blue, invalid,
but not unwelcome sky, lit like a hotel sign.

To the New World

What eats through fibers, salt
And sting, our hands defeat.
We make our journey comforting—
Wood masts rot, or is it just

That planks reflect the gutter light
Of daybreak? Dawns we wake
To smoke of rusted galley stoves.
From buckets, swabbing hieroglyphs,

The story going on the wall.
Our prayer: Consume
My heart away. The seaman's
Cough, the first mate shrill.

Brass canteen, directory and quills
Coursing under foam, holds
Stocked with flour, rosaries.
We keep the books. We keep

And write it down, and look
For tell-tale signs.
An albatross. Whale whiteness
In the sky. The bleakness

Of our tarnished boat, the afterglows
Of beach. A voyage
We've been on so long.
But weren't we spoken to?

These rocking waves, vast winds.
No laws. Not here.
No laws, no hearth, no heart,
No dowry dress, we mean no harm.

II

Name Desire

Monarch, like a tuning fork struck,
latches to a deaf ear, spent.

Chinese lantern swinging
from a milkweed.

The playwright christens you
Blanche, which you do,

coquettishly. Who can help us?
I am waiting for the gallows.

I am waiting for the bolt.
Uneven-fingered mighty seasons.

Bangles on the oak leaf and the blight.

First a rumble, always the arrival
of the cart. Wings unravel giant

vistas, butterfly, in the hand.

Akhmatova to her Husband in Russia

Modigliani paints me spire-like
with roses, yellow buds. He crouches
with his brush. I recline, my bangs like tips
of granite, stilettoed dark beneath my brows.
I will learn to count on no one. He purchases
more paint. How spare, this world,
before the literati. How easy to emerge
from worn-out pillows, charcoal sketches,
symbols, poems. You have your past, a heart
carved in Petersburg. Painters struggle,
unlike you. I like freedom too. Now I begin,
while skaters preen on the lake. Their blades
shimmer silver, blue, as Modigliani
scribbles, tracks a vein from mouth to arm,
the wing of my brow, the odor of roses.

Odysseus with a Siren in the Corner of His Eye

What are you afraid of? You'll see her
gleaming from the cave, her stare,

stony, unreadable. By ear you navigate
your cruel way home, short of breath.

Walls along the crypts,
a chorus on the shore, spikes of glass

track the ridge. What is it in her words,
frozen grains opening melodically

like tiny grates. The nautilus.
Admit it: your grizzled eye

is pleased. You hoped for
salt flats, white beach, dead sleep,

the grotto where she's not supposed to be.
You can't have everything. The veins

in your arm swell, stoked
by wind, blue on the prow.

Do you know you're angry?

Russian Chapter

What's fated is the game hen,
the dish of praline dusted in sugar,
servants in rust-red coats,
the big house open for wounded.
An army bottlenecks behind
its horse-backed lieutenants.

Deserters call and wave their sacks
at the carriage bound for Petersburg.
A plump bird in a furry hat,
the young man dreams his unknown wife
he'll meet four years down the road
who now plays cards in Paris.

Halo

I have freshly painted walls,
bare except the painting of the children
hanging lanterns. In the morning,
polished oils lift me and at night.

Outside, these patterns still reflect
the blank exhaust from jets
that shout beneath a dislocating sun.
My unkempt lookout is the bed,

azaleas, their flamenco heads
beyond the cat's reach. On the rooftop,
burning slate, or the image of burning
behind your picture, unsubdued.

Proverb

A room with a roof is all bed
as you are bed, botanical gardens, breath
on the face. A room with no roof
in low cloud, dissolves in smoke,
the lone mound in the field, and the worst
kind offers collect. The road defrocks you.

The Way Light Travels

In brackish light,
the horn,
the bird-like twitch
of trolley.

Absently,
you press me.
The mindless roll
down metal track.

It's the shape,
the noise cars make
around a small girl's
room at night,

the way light
travels, mouthing one sound.
She lies quiet.
It will pass again.

Flare of yellow
on the yellow wall.
The movement,
footless,

Ash Wednesday
when soot
stains the forehead
like a headlight.

Dirt clings to heat
of Sister's skin,
beads, fades.
Children mark their books.

The girl looks up,
wants someone
to share this with.
Where did it come from?

Where will it go?
Buttonhole,
a black cloak.
Outside, dank hyacinth.

The Nymphs, Seeing Circe at the Table

Change, for nymphs, is essential. Here we eat clams
in the sun, crack them in our hooves.

Our island is windy. We're raked by tropic weather.
You sit at Circe's table, palms spread,

flaring like a sow. You snuffle for your dinner.
Your sweet hands are more than she can bear.

They mutter towards her body the way ivy licks
the walls of our bordello; the little shock

of dampness gives color. She gives you
figs, wine, pipes, pear-skin flesh.

The hands on her body are human.
Like the ivy, inflammations

never start without this give and take.
She screens her knowledge,

her methods of living. No one is trusted.
She loves her animals and wants to eat them.

Song for the Oarsman

River of amber, moss river
rowers sidle, children sell
fried dough, bouquets, or play guitar.
The ride is smooth, no waves.

Canal of flowers, music canal
starboard, someone's taken a picture,
possibly the best one ever, all lit,
the boat's name woven in flowers.

River of amber, moss river
on both sides, jungle tangles,
snails in ivy, a superhighway
speeds off from the floodbank.

Canal of flowers, music canal
the boy in back with a pole
shoves us down the quiet hall of water
seated on our wooden bench.

The Kiss

    after Caravaggio's *The Taking of Christ*

Nothing flickers from the lantern, even though it glows.
Christ leans away, although you say he's leaning forward,
the metalled arm, a fulcrum between pans.

A light, you're right, comes from elsewhere.
They look at him or look away. The crowd's not looking
as he folds into himself, or at the fingers which hover and sting,
sick of gesturing. Only he can feel their breath

and you, so sharp, you know
that only our light reflects off their bodies,
the weight of the glove at his neck.

Speak Back

Akhmatova writes a lyric on asps,
no place to go but her own arms,
while she sits typing, typing, and nights pass,
one syllable beaten in ice.
She clutches a brick in bed for the heat,
snow puffing the panes. Like Narcissus,
she wants the water to look back.
What is it about silence, Rilke asks.
His years without words, angels and heartbreaks
lost in German architecture.

Someone once told me I'd be ashamed
of what I write—what it's like
to walk on gravestones,
shuffle down sidewalks. The world,
a hull, beckons, takes my confidence away.
Its fabric is empty. I'm looking for a shirt
to fit in—skies and cars, grey
in all directions, flat, humid, no rain.
Boston, grey stones under the elms,
wearing its frills. Prudential,
North Station, North End,

and in the pizza place across the street
the old man at the table
talking how *nobody treat me that way*,
the woman staring back at him vacantly.
Don't want another Thanksgiving like that,
another New Year's. The only thing
saved me was work. Was seeing you.
The furnace hissing on. I keep thinking about it.

Letters from an Exile

Trotsky's dead. My strays
crouch in bed. All night,
cup after cup from the samovar,
end of the revolution,
the cat tail's twitch. This
is how I melt the glacier,
chisel out the past. *Comrade,
we thought we could set them all free.*
If I were still welcome,
you'd be here. Marx was important,
rights were important.
If I were still welcome.

*Comrade, old clothing
stuffed under the door,*
I talk to myself about
world events. Rinse the face,
move lamp from desk to shelf to desk,
shorn neck, skullcap tied tight
to the bone. I'm gazing
at your photograph.

Why I write is beyond me.
Go to sleep. Extracting
ticks and brush from our hair, evenings
in the settlement, remember?
We painted and cooked,
walked barefoot, remember?
We argue and sweat.

The Road to Hell is Paved with

Apology.

Dear heart,
A steady hand passed over the color of fields
as they were, red spike of a flower again and again like spokes
    of a wheel,
roads limed with mist. I was too busy watching the field to feel
anything but cold glass, the track, too stunned to believe,
unable to express the difficulty. In the speed
of the train and our second-hand clothes, you murmured,
What's love there? When we cross the continents, I told you, *we'll
Trap our own dinner, thaw by the kettle.*

Dear cage,
Like music, you changed my appearance, how I lived,
    my strange ways.
When I find myself complaining,
I walk through the woods, dragging tragically
through underbrush. Coils of yellowjackets, watersnakes,
    distinctions we made:
factory heat from a frigid rail, uranium turning dirt to glass.
    The desert
sky, soft voices of half-lives, periodic,
like people, resistant to probe. I watched a storm come that
    afternoon, almost striking
a house, then packed up and left, black as the station was
    spreading its light.

Dear life,
The lack of water never let me rest. Unable to think you knew
    of my need
…on all sides, the landscape bloomed like a cottonfield
    (why couldn't you leave
me alone)…unable to give you the benefit of knowing anything
at all, I thought I saw you look back, I thought
that I was the one who was vulnerable.

Tornado Alley

On the backstairs, empty bottles quiver
and wait. Dakota sky knits itself gray
while Etta James belts the blues,
senses the promiscuous rain,
no end in sight. This midwest crisis builds
like a train. The record repeats its lyrical
theme on a rusted box. Who could be bothered
to love now? The wind, spider-like and low,
blows webs across the crusted windowpane.
The land blackens. Blackberries bulge,
heavy-headed and pained, at the storm's
approach. The letter I wrote. The needle's stuck
and underbrush leaps at the window
as if we could escape unscratched.

Kept

They move like twins, the Siamese
sliced neatly from the butcher's block.
Through corridors called house
and home, burrowers
make meanings for themselves
between themselves with fierceness even
children know.

The French say paramour,
clearly derived, sex *par
amour*. It's livery
I have no patience for:
servant clothes, feudal lords.
As if a part of grade school. Scents
of boots, coats, boatlike mops
twisted in locked closets,
ammonia smells and paint.

A child chants prayer wheels,
coupled with another, grasped
by arms, eyes closed, spun
faster, faster. Buddy system
chained in two.
Who loves, who holds you there? One
more turn before
she begs release, the blacktop voices
shrieking, in their new white shoes.

    First rate, he said, first rate
    commodity, hair like yours
    so thick you might forget
    you accepted the apology...

First more than one,
then less, then
never sure, hand to hand.
A rose behind an ear,
between the teeth, your place in line
behind the tall girl, boy
who pulls her ponytail, whispers

near her ear, inside
the way shell rushes sea by drum and bone,
Do you like me? Do you like me now?
Unattached, the other half,
a story you make up yourself

some childhood joke, the body prize and tool.

George Sand's Invitation to Her Lover

As a child, I told the sun to rise
and he did, stretched himself like a pale god
across the sky to warm me,
glad to be called.
I was dark, cloaked,
even under the sun.
My invitation was our secret.

Since then I have grown and shaped myself.
I slide into faces and forms:
an author in the cafe,
a man of stature
strutting down the streets,
the leopard in the drawing room,
taciturn and bold as snow.

It is winter and I watch for you.
On a cold, Gothic day like this
I am most alive, as expectant and unsure
as the words which rush from me at dawn.
My hands clutched by my sides hurt
as if submerged in ice. They burn.

You do not know what to make of me.
I am mercurial and flushed. I will never be
a simple angel, ethereal or spring-like.
You come to see your troubadour, your George.
You make your tracks,
an animal across the frozen ground.

Urban Blue

Some are drawn to fire, to bondage,
some finger the heart like an organ.
You like a breed to lick you with an
ox-like tongue. You're offering something:
a rope, a cube, a safe place to sleep.
I want you to stand in my way.
You take walks in the dark to find me.
Buildings look inward when I pass, shades
drawn. Capacity for love and loneliness
an old ballad on my chest. The smell
of you on my clothes is like the words
you said. The country I come from. The homeless
shape we made. I am only here in passing: sunset
on the skyline, white sheets, your rocking chair.

Little Opera

I need bright paints, high sound
to distract me. Oils stain my hands.
Muffled elevator charging—gates
snap, echo down the hall. Language
of the brush. Voices, records, bobbing.
Mozart's diva quivers on the turntable.
A fern decays on the white sill, dirty
corners chipped. Volume of the male
bird. The downpour lows against the wall.
Thrashed maples. Windows slam
above wet trees. You're gone for good.
Wind-filled branches watered a cappella.
Paint and turmoil. Stern, electric
gems, women singing in my presence.

Manhattan

What's so terrible about disappearing? The wedding bower was covered in sunflowers and large red lilies. Children were assumed of this union. The chuppah from the bride's side, the goblet, knocked over by the Rabbi, from the groom's. A rustling of attendants, and everywhere parents and parents of parents who ever held a wedding in synagogue or gallery, by the rivers of Babylon, like this one. At the reception, the violinist and pianist dueled Bartok fiercely. We got drunk and ate in the library. Actors, publishers, museum curates called for town cars. Soon the return to Queens down Roosevelt Ave under the El, rap on the radio, with men clandestine on the streets beside the shuttered shops. There were oysters in the Roosevelt Hotel before boarding the train, as we walked beneath Grand Central's crystal constellations to the lobby through the automatic doors. Dwarfed by then, for no good reason other than departure, flanked by metal, stone. Dusk never fully takes hold, everyone's lights on and the endless yellow taxis bloom.

III

Legend

This is what it was like: woods full of children,
thickets and pockets for them to climb into and hide,
tired of victim, assassin, tired of leaving their
bread crumbs behind like parts of their lives,
a hand, a thigh, some feelings disgorged—limbs,
emotions, stud the broken path like ghosts
and the children wander as if from the sea,
the ancient mist, mythic, deepens and whitens
around them until each one stands in front of a man
with the mouth of a wolf, he calls to them, traps them;
their world (you must understand) rips and tears
like his flesh, as they wheel each time into safety,
his bottomless belly, he drags them into his forest
grove, they always go, willing.

Lughnasa

Tiny lanterns flutter on oil rigs.
Sails wrap the mast and pull for Wales.
Water comes in. Shadows of reeds hit the sill.

Levels rise, the sea a mirror. Blackthorn scrapes
back and forth, rides against ground that pulls,
shrinks away. Everything resists.

The people of Dun Laoghaire settle in, the wind
gentle or seizing the window.

One minute, beach, another, sea.
                    Kingstownies are impenetrable.
Water makes its way up the strand.

A boy at home paints landscapes, ruins his eyes,
considers great beginnings, the genesis of tides.
He balances a book, held like china
then runs off to watch
the tinker's fire in his hideout by the dunes.

The Curator Explains

It's hard to see
country festivity when watching the road,
the hedges close in on the left.

Weather-wrapped, the body
takes a sheen, a camouflage
while village hands hell-bent on the cleaning

of bones prepare the bricks
of the monastic cell, the muck
that will preserve you.

Strangers eye fern-covered
hewn and minted digits,
hint of fountain pennies in the basin,

whitewashed, rattling requiems as we pass
the summer grass. You, tucked
in your pallet, a closed current.

They can guess
your story if they're bored.
Fished from the bog,

brought back blind, boxed under glass
in the National. No restorative for this.
You look like ambivalence

caught in headlights,
old flickers. There's no question
I don't have to

like you or anyone.
Sometimes all judgmental tribes and their wives
get to do is tilt their head and smile and read the placard.

The Ferry North to Isle of Mull

I think of conversations heard on board, how little
mail contains, my skin
bristling in the wind. Think of myself most of all—
who would I talk to back in Glasgow?
The postcard jotted to the States: "I broke
for Mull today....It's early June..." How can one grasp
a continent away the highland rocks that pocket
in my fist?
The water's crossbow slits, the reeds' backlash.
Volcanic plots grow heavy in the wrists.

Gospel

It's over sketch and color
of an evangelist's eyes,
a robe's red hem
that he toils,
graphs the heart's
condition.
A Book of Kells is ready,

lord, with breath.
Sun lattices
the road of text,
dust on bodies
bent, defending letters
from the honeycomb
the draught of ale. The taste
of nubbled metal,

tongue to screen.
Saints burst their boxes
under flint they weather
at his hands. He pens
serpents, lions, snaps
on corsets, herbs,
crosses, nail heads.
Crickets perch

with emerald crests
on Latin words
in the field of lapis
lazuli, white lead.
A gold and copper tree line fire
glows, the script
illuminating bedposts.
Patchwork pupils tunnel

within vowels, the choir
nestles. In cloistered bath,
moist forehead to the netting
of a palm, he thinks he hears
a note, can't wait

to draw it. Bright
hemoglobin of crushed insects,
vellum fingered
and placed back.

Viking

The old Norse heaves electric heat,
and breaks its spines against the pane.
I want to pick and spear what's difficult,
to nestle the space heater,
stay in bed renouncing Iceland.

After bathing, dripping on the carpet,
battened like a boat or animal,
I want to tame what's mineral
and mine, a great vowel shift,

dry air across a lava field. How warm
that day would be.
The chrome bores on and once
you're in, you're in.

Waterfront

Nothing to see but seagulls stiff,
still buffeted, like traffic.
They're immortal either way.
The peddler by the quay

fights a cold, wonders if his girl
rankles just like him,
clears his throat at the black water,
thinks, "she'll be sleeping well

where she's gone."
The grocer with his leg in plaster
puts out artichokes, and laughs,
hand on his apron: "I'm no good

at being alone."
Two friends eat mussels
in the shop, dig them with the shell
and loiter by the fire, fueled

by rumor. Awnings flirt across the docks.
A street musician stalls with frost.
The river-wind arranges us
and shapes us in a blunt-cut bowl.

Tell You

To the closeness of you, I give up my body
You are well-rested
Here I am older than you

I will tell you something
I am a night person, medicated
in your bed   We live alone

in a public place and have deceived each other
I want to pay for my crimes
I am waiting to be turned into nightingale

So many men take your face now
I am excommunicated
You have simply loved me

too long   Understand
I am fucking Salinger as often as you
I want to be looked in the eyes

Before the Monks, Attempts at Confession

Consider this first—The message on display
unraveling like script in the half-light,
I rub my foot along the wood as if facing straight
meant suffering and looking up would put me

out to sea. Altars chafe the iron body
on the grate, mottled (as I am). Secluded,
spice on our lips, the cook's breath. Silent
as the fire goes out. The anxious blue

of their eyes, blackcloth and devotion. A lump of candle
sweats against my fingers, dropcloth and pews.
Bright with noise, I weep as a child weeps,
fists wrapped in hair. Binding wounds, scrawled illegibly *feel it*

as I do across the monastery floor, the hand is warm,
the hand I meant to save—*not incapable of abandon.*

The Mill Wheel

The last gables fade off the street.
I count up my failures, gaze at my nails,
the wolf rolls from my mouth,
bares his teeth—
we love this as much as we hate it.
Alone, we walk to the park.

Relief comes in a place that's not
ours, on a bench, dogs barking. Down the street,
a ball is tossed again and again
on the side of house, the heart's thud.
He's got eyes that look through me

to treadmills, the mule's
dead circle, steps lightly.
Battalions and bayonets,
thoughts threading the chaos and sulphur
of me. Deep in it, we're wolves,

checking out people. We stick together.
At least we have each other,
never sleep, have difficulty forgetting.
We know all the shopkeepers' names.
I put my fists out
and hope I hit something.

He asks why I'm blind now.
The walls rust each afternoon,
tints in the wood are crows,
a necklace, a light shaft,
a glass with water in it,

a green swath of forest,
bright sun, all I've seen.
Roads, the arrows shot at birds,
sacred places, old haunts.
The slaughter of cows in England.
The light the shades keep out.

Illness Makes an Agreeable Variety

Like mottled skin, the sky uncertain:
sun or rain? The light an ochre
spring soil thaw, the day of Keats'
hemorrhage. Attention slips,
not to poems, sister, chair
with splintered back, starched
sheet, cat upon the footstool,
staring. Not regret
of travel in July, the letters
clustered on his desk,
not Shakespeare in the parlor,
no fleeting thought, pathology
or flush, of cells' uproar,
or chest sweat. He tastes
copper in his teeth, yeast
from the pantry, hears the horse in paddock's
counterpoint to Charles' instruction
shouted from the door. Beyond,
the washerwoman's curls and scalloped edge
of her cloche as she runs. His eye
on a slightly tilted charcoal sketch.
Years and illness come to this,
he casts his net:
When I said to Brown "this is unfortunate,"
I thought of you. Tis true
that since the first two or three days
other subjects have entered my head.

The Shepherd

They jump the stone, they
clamber up the rock face, mewl
funereally on top. I climb up
to comfort them (the country never ends,
no walls can hold the sheep), then rude,
sling them on my back and swing them down.

Women I know are all the same.
No longing. Snapping joints.
If one were stranded on the cliff,
she'd parachute her great arms
and flatten me. My girls will bury me
one day with their broad shanks
thinking they will keep me warm.

If they nuzzle or chew at my corpse
I will be the centerpiece of sacredness.

The shed out back fills with rain.
If I could find a woman to give all
my love, I would feed her
what's now sought by my sweet ladies,
thick hips, no minds, great grief
in their eyes. I know the call

that keeps them, the smack on the flank,
the intimate whisper, the coveted cliché.

View on the Arno: Coming About

after a painting by Thomas Cole

Explain immersion, watch the cashmere sun
extend to edge and vanish so the captain
says. Across the floor, we spot another mast.
A green hull pulls against the drag, where bodies
brushed on boats patrol like swans. They're almost
us. We overlap. In this world, real or psychological,
life's fuzzy toward the shore. The plot of water stiffens
while we wait, slurred and faceless, tight inside the boat.
Land-trapped relations wave us in to sleep—a moon
to stretch across—to cottonwood, weeds that fringe
the frame, stake the wall. Flax. Curl and swag, green
between shores, resistant.
Note: we like it here, we like the birds
that never sing but watch us.

Year after Year

a brief beach
   the bare run
and shell thrust in scuff
   imprinted paper thin
a brief beach
   the bare run
off the path from the park
   my bevel, my bench
and beyond, a corner
   capstone, glove shaped,
my bevel, my bench
   and on the sweating
capstone, glove shaped
   seaweed crusted
embedded ceramic
   in a ruined village
or panhandler's camp

Brooklyn

American Epic? You mean from the ferry,
bridges lit up for the night? When I take off my glasses,
strung deck beads ignite. Pigeons walk inside. A boy
pulls his cap to his eyes: Mother was a haberdasher's daughter
and father met her out on Coney Island.
Everyone's drifting. Apartment's filled with children,
pilot lights are out, clothes strewn,
curtains left unwashed. We're led from the water-
front to huddle on the bow. First, second, third child,
fourth, fifth, clutching our smudged bodies, we're a country,
calling ourselves immigrants. We cull provisions
on the boat. Lifejackets under the seats. Mistake?
I never called us that. Resented? I never imagined.

Composition

In the Symphony district, one man thumbs
the storm sonata, any sonata,

from the stone bench, undoes his scarf
The language we know and looks

into the pit's black mouth. Sewers
plume with smoke behind the festival. He sees

them steam steady in the street,
can hear the crowd, their screams.

To put the heart. *Half a pitch*
he thinks, plays C, E, G.

Young boys leap the chain-link fence, stuck
to wires. *Put the heart*

Hands scab and heal. One small hood in each palm,
fussing beneath the bandage. Nothing

comes of it. Each year, they've barbs,
coins, the fence to scale. Always a girl,

still high school, the center of attention,
all lips and chords, an emanation:

streetlight, lodestone, candle, sky. Image and lie.
Play as if she were Words we forget, he sighs,

forgetting. *Many ways*
to say His own mind drowned in sharps

and flats. Piano, singer, gesture. Alleys
from cobbles from silt. *I live* He could have said

something human. Lively strings.
There are many ways to say the thing.

Critical

All those gadgets clear obstructions
of the airway. Some people died in here.
Can't look. The bulb's half gone, no one
sees a thing. In the other room a woman
sobs into a towel. Steam billows
from a nozzle. The company wanders in
off the streets. Light's a comfort, movement's comfort.
One's arms could go right through,
nothing holds us. A homeless man says
acid's in his drink. Maybe someone wants
to kill him. Talk goes on all night. Blood
flutters in an ear. I can't read anymore,
our regrets. *Get the hell out of here. Go on.*

Recess

Children in pink and tawny coats hurl the ball at one another, screaming. Some throw their arms wide and pitch obscenities. The lot is empty except for these bodies jerking back and forth. A boy with yellow hair and gummy shoes puts his face against the bars and yells to the dog by the curb. If the dog were a boy, he'd have yellow hair and gummy shoes, and the same military disposition. Some kids are speaking Haitian Creole, or steam-rolling their vowels in distinct South Boston. A few speak Korean. The school is spray painted beneath feet leaping and arching to dodge the ball. Breath plumes visibly. Corrupt sound still moves. Put your hand on the pulse in my neck as I mouth the words.

Intaglio

I want to check myself in,
say I'm here, let's begin,
I'm not sure how to start,
where to go. First snow.

First flurry, hardness
of my collarbone,
first I've noticed, envious
of mobility in this world.

We lie still for sex,
momentary glitter;
in my head, this connection,
untouchable: *quaint rings,
intaglios, amethysts...*

back to Henry James, laced
in fiction. This book, windowpane,
ice, the sheer wealth of it,
or the ending of *Notorious*:
Grant wipes the stairs with Bergman,
saves her from the Nazis.

Practically dead, a poison-clogged drain,
what matters in her stupor is familiar,
his eyes on her, his shoes,
light trussed in iris, patent leather.

It reveals what could
feel good about dishonesty.
Love, *Great Gatsbied*.
The East Egg sun. The terrycloth robe
that hides the cracks.
If you stay, come morning, then

Look at yourself. Bones, white
and hard. This drifting is so odd,
pre-rehearsed on marble floor.
Now, separate flights. Over dark
sky, a letter breaking open in descent.
I can see the ocean.
I can see us falling in the water.

The Booby

In fall sunlight, exposed,
suddenly strong again—there.
Blue-footed. If you've ever been to Ecuador,
you'll note the feet
aren't sky or indigo,
pigments pure aqua or deep
orange as Rothko dreams
a luminous spread. Not cadmium,
but pulsar, deep-hued, slightly blue
grainy boots
sink into white-hot lava as it cools.
One foot billows, blankets

the cipher. Truth is, I'm caught
off-guard, having forgotten
what I love is certain: this step, that step,
a catch in the lung, coughed incessantly
as it all dies out. And I want it
to die out. The bird is just part pelican,
part circus-freak. For some reason God
chose the feet as a sign of His Wit.

The name thrown in to contradict
as I reach into the feathered breast
experiencing brief life and death. Unless
I teach the awkward bird
what I like with those coveted webs.
Lift one, then the other, dumb
drawbridge. Adoringly
a foot waves in.

It's easier with a model, wings
fresh and stiff from taxidermy.
Almost out of mind, easily exploited,

under wraps. You simply leave
the room when it dies.
A change of scene at the break.
Nothing terrifies. I'm saying

walls jut and shift in fall sunlight
the way we jut and shift before we die.
Under raiment, cipher.

I know for sure
I've never seen one
real as rain clatters off the side of the house.
Such images turn keepsake,
fit in the top drawer. A hole with plush overtones
absorbs everything, everything. Everything
goes. Adjust. The truth is this:

My image razed, a woman made
of books but with a core that radiates,
then flickers, then goes out,
the flames. Nobody seething
but that bird, that bird. Those blinding feet.

And it is said:
of all that's left, these islands are
partitioned off, braced, fire-lit.
Blue footed, strange

and many species flourished there.

Author Biography

Valerie Duff is the poetry editor for Salamander Magazine, and she has received St. Botolph and Massachusetts Cultural Council grants for her poetry. She earned her masters degree in creative writing from Boston University and Trinity College, Dublin. Her poems have appeared in *Ploughshares, Harvard Review, PN Review AGNI, Zoland Poetry: an Annual of Poems, Translations and Interviews*, and elsewhere; her book reviews have appeared in *Salamander, Bostonia*, and *PN Review*. Her short play, "The Means Which Enable Me to Work," was performed in an Arlington New Plays Festival in 2004. Valerie is a freelance writer and editor for Bedford/St. Martin's Press. She lives in Boston with her husband and two children.